IMAGES
of Aviation

NORTH DAKOTA
AIR NATIONAL GUARD

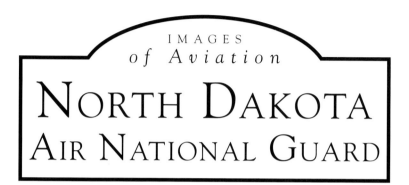

IMAGES
of Aviation

NORTH DAKOTA
AIR NATIONAL GUARD

David Lipp and Maxwell Sabin

ARCADIA
PUBLISHING

Published by Arcadia Publishing
Charleston, South Carolina

Printed in the United States of America

Library of Congress Control Number: 2022948260

For all general information, please contact Arcadia Publishing:
Telephone 843-853-2070
Fax 843-853-0044
E-mail sales@arcadiapublishing.com
For customer service and orders:
Toll-Free 1-888-313-2665

Visit us on the Internet at www.arcadiapublishing.com

*To the men and women of the North Dakota Air National Guard
who have served and who are currently serving.*

CONTENTS

ACKNOWLEDGMENTS

All of the images from the World War II chapter came from the collections at the National Archives in Washington, DC, as noted. One photograph of the C-47 "Minnie H" at Bonanzaville was taken by author Maxwell Sabin. The remainder of the images in this book were taken by professional photographers of the North Dakota Air National Guard while doing their duty. Many of these photographs have never been published.

INTRODUCTION

Although the Army National Guard can trace its history to more than 100 years before the founding of the United States, the history of the Air National Guard (ANG) is fairly new. The earliest squadrons within the Air Guard were founded during and just after World War I. These squadrons were attached to the local Army National Guard units as observation and pursuit squadrons. During World War II, many of these early Air Guard units were called up for active duty for tasks such as training, maritime patrol, and transport. Following the end of World War II, the Air Force became a separate branch of the military outside of the Army. This was at a time when the need for continental air defense was high. The threat of Soviet invasion or attack was real, and to counter this, the US Air Force (USAF) developed interceptor squadrons within the newly founded Air National Guard to help counter this threat. Among the newly founded squadrons was the 178th Fighter Squadron (FS), assigned to the North Dakota Air National Guard.

The lineage of the 178th FS can be traced back to the 392nd Fighter Squadron during World War II. The 392nd FS was attached to the 367th Fighter Group of the 9th US Air Force. During the war, the 392nd flew missions in the P-38 Lightning and P-47 Thunderbolt in the European Theater. The 392nd saw some of its most intense combat in the weeks following the D-Day invasion, where they were responsible for cutting off German supplies to the front lines. The squadron was awarded a Distinguished Unit Citation in August 1944 for destroying five German convoys and roughly one hundred tanks in a single day. The highest-scoring ace of the 367th FG was Larry "Scrappy" Blumer. Blumer was a native of Kindred, North Dakota, and is credited as being the "fastest ace in a day" in the entire US Army Air Forces (USAAF). On August 25, 1944, Blumer shot down five German Focke-Wulf 190 fighters in a span of 15 minutes. He was the commander of the 392nd FS from November 1944 to January 1945. By the time he returned to the United States, Blumer had amassed a total of six confirmed kills with a seventh probable. The 392nd FS finished the war with 39.5 confirmed kills, the most of any of the three squadrons in "the Dynamite Gang." The 392nd was deactivated on November 7, 1945.

The growing tensions of the Cold War forced the newly founded USAF to reactivate many of the World War II–era squadrons that had been disbanded at the war's end. Among them was the 392nd, which had been allotted to the ANG in 1946 and was redesignated the 178th Fighter Squadron. The first fighter aircraft assigned to the 178th were P-51D Mustangs, which were later redesignated as F-51s when the USAF dropped the "P" for pursuit in 1947. Many of the original 178th FS F-51 Mustang pilots had been pilots during World War II. Among them was Duane "Pappy" Larson. During the war, Pappy flew with the 504th FS, 339th Fighter Group (FG) flying the P-51 from RAF (Royal Air Force) Fowlmere in England. He flew 68 combat missions and was awarded the Distinguished Flying Cross before returning home in November 1944. In addition to the F-51D Mustang, the 178th FS also flew the AT-6 Texan, B-26 Invader, B-25 Mitchell, C-45 Expeditor, and C-47 Skytrain as operational support aircraft in the first 10 years of the NDANG's history. The NDANG flew the F-51 until 1954, when it transitioned to the Lockheed F-94A/B interceptor, the first jet aircraft for the NDANG. The F-94A/Bs were still armed with large-caliber machine guns, but in April 1957, the unit received the all-new F-94C Starfire variant, featuring unguided air-to-air rockets and an advanced radar that could work in tandem with the newly installed Semi-Automatic Ground Environment (SAGE) system in the late 1950s. During this time, the NDANG produced the first aircrew that qualified in an all-weather rocket-firing aircraft in the entire Air National Guard. The NDANG flew the F-94C until 1960, when it transitioned to the Northrop F-89 Scorpion.

The F-89 Scorpion brought new challenges to the NDANG as it became the first unit in the ANG to serve on 24-hours-a-day, seven-days-a-week nuclear alert. This required NDANG air and ground crews to be prepared to scramble at a moment's notice. The first F-89 variants assigned to the NDANG were the F-89D; however, they were quickly supplemented and ultimately replaced by the nuclear-capable F-89J Scorpion. Although the Scorpion may not have been the fastest or best-looking jet flown by the NDANG, it holds a special spot in the hearts of many NDANG members as it was the first mission aircraft to bear the world-famous "Happy Hooligans" nickname. The Happy Hooligans participated in the 1964 Ricks Trophy, holding first place throughout the event until the final day. The Ricks Trophy was the USAF's initial precursor to the Aerial Gunnery Weapons Competition, also known as William Tell. The 1964 competition was the Hooligans' first visit to Tyndall for the competition and certainly was not the last. The last of the NDANG F-89J Scorpions were reassigned to other units in 1966, being replaced by the supersonic F-102A Delta Dagger.

The first F-102 Delta Daggers assigned to the Happy Hooligans arrived in September 1966. Referred to by its fliers as a "pilot's dream," the supersonic F-102A and its unique side-by-side trainer version, the TF-102A, were the first supersonic aircraft flown by the NDANG. During the F-102 era of the late 1960s, the NDANG had its first dual-role commander. Davenport, North Dakota, native Alexander "Mac" Macdonald became the 119th Fighter Group commander in February 1968 and held the position until September 1974. He became the dual-role commander in February 1968, when he was appointed base detachment commander. The Happy Hooligans were the only ANG unit to receive the flying safety award for the 1968 calendar year—the unit's second such award since 1959. The F-102 era for the NDANG was not without its lows, however. "Minnie H," the faithful C-47A Skytrain that had been assigned to the NDANG in 1947, was retired from service in 1969 after an illustrious career with both the USAAF in World War II and the NDANG. Its replacement was the Douglas C-54 Skymaster. On November 18, 1968, during a flight back to North Dakota from Springfield, Illinois, the C-54 lost its No. 3 engine mid-flight while carrying North Dakota governor Bill Guy and his wife. Remarkably, the quick reactions of the flight crew saved the aircraft and the lives of all on board. The following year, however, the C-54 was lost over Alaska with all hands on board going down with it. Among them was Lt. Col. Donald Flesland, 178th Fighter-Interceptor Squadron commander. The wreckage of the C-54 was not found until 1972, almost three years from the day of its disappearance. The F-102, while one of the fastest aircraft the Happy Hooligans ever flew, was also the shortest lived with the unit. In 1969, the Happy Hooligans transitioned from the F-102A to the F-101 Voodoo.

The NDANG was one of the first Air National Guard interceptor squadrons to receive the F-101 Voodoo after they were transferred from active duty interceptor units. The NDANG proved that it was one of the best F-101B Voodoo units in the USAF with the sheer amount of awards it won during the "Voodoo era" from 1969 to 1977. The Happy Hooligans were put to the test less than a year after they received the F-101 when they attended the 1970 USAF biennial weapons competition. Despite going against Canadian, active duty Air Force and other ANG squadrons, the Happy Hooligans emerged victorious from William Tell, coming in first place in the F-101B category and taking home the "Top Gun" award, which was awarded to NDANG captains James Reimers and Arthur Jacobson for being the best pilot/weapon-system officer (WSO) team in the competition. The Hooligans made history in 1972 when they again won first place in the F-101B category, becoming the first Air National Guard squadron to accomplish such a feat. In 1974, the NDANG became the first ANG squadron to receive the Hughes Trophy, awarded to the best

USAF Air Defense Squadron in the early 1950s and now known as the Raytheon Achievement Trophy. The Happy Hooligans were awarded the 1974 Daedalian Maintenance Trophy, becoming the first unit in history to win both the Hughes Trophy and Daedalian Maintenance Trophy in the same year. In October 1976, the NDANG was the first squadron in the Air National Guard to send a woman member to pilot training. Beach, North Dakota, native 2nd Lt. Marilyn Koon was selected from the NDANG. Unfortunately, due to USAF rules at the time, she could not fly combat aircraft, so she transferred to the Arizona ANG and became a KC-135 pilot with the 161st Aerial Refueling Group. In 1977, the NDANG retired its F-101s and replaced them with the iconic F-4D Phantom II.

The North Dakota ANG flew the venerable F-4D Phantom II from 1977 to 1990. During the "F-4 era," the Happy Hooligans had their first overseas deployment to Naval Air Station Keflavik, Iceland, in 1984. During this deployment, Hooligan F-4 aircrews intercepted eight Soviet Tu-95 "Bear" long-range bombers. During the 1984 William Tell competition in September of that year, the Happy Hooligan load team took first place in the F-4 category, and in the following competition in 1986, came in first place overall in the F-4 category. In 1986, the Hooligans were part of the first Air National Guard rotation to assume the USAF Zulu alert mission at Ramstein Air Base (AB), West Germany. Referred to as "Creek Klaxon," aircraft and personnel from the North Dakota; Duluth, Minnesota; and Fresno, California, Air National Guard units rotated to Ramstein and stood on continuous alert for one year, providing air sovereignty in Western Europe for NATO during the waning years of the Cold War. The F-4 era also saw many iconic leaders of the Happy Hooligans. In 1981, longtime NDANG member Col. Thornton "Beck" Becklund assumed command of the 119th Fighter Intercept Group (FIG), replacing Col. Alexander "Mac" Macdonald, who went on to become the North Dakota adjutant general. In 1983, Lt. Col. Wally Hegg assumed command of the 119th FIG. The final commander of the 119th FIG during the F-4 era was Col. Gary Kaiser, who assumed command from Lieutenant Colonel Hegg in April 1987. In October 1989, the Hooligans began their alert detachment at Kingsley Field, Oregon, which would last until 1994. In December 1989, the 119th Security Police Flight was named the best security police in the entire Air National Guard. In early 1990, the last of the Happy Hooligans' F-4Ds were retired to the Aerospace Maintenance and Regeneration Center in Tucson, Arizona, known as the boneyard, and the unit's final fighter aircraft, the F-16A Fighting Falcon, became operational.

The Happy Hooligans received their first F-16As in January 1990. The variants that were assigned to the NDANG were no ordinary F-16s, but older variants that had been upgraded specifically for Air National Guard units in the early 1990s. The air defense variant featured advanced Identify Friend or Foe (IFF) equipment, a Bendix-King AN/ARC-200 high-frequency single-sideband radio, and a 150,000-candlepower night identification spotlight installed on the port side. The Hooligan air-defense fighter (ADF) F-16s were all uniquely outfitted to carry radar-guided missiles (AIM-7), an identification light mounted on the port side for night visual identification (VID), specialized intercept geometry software for night, all-weather intercepts and IDs, on-board IFF, and an HF radio for long-range communications. No other F-16s had these features except the ADF variants. Col. Michael Hagen assumed command of the 119th Fighter-Interceptor Group in 1992 and served as the commander until 1999. He was the North Dakota adjutant general from 2000 through 2006, following Maj. Gen. Keith Bjerke, who served as the adjutant general from 1993 through 2000. In 1994, the Happy Hooligans competed in the William Tell competition. They came in first overall and were the first F-16 unit in the USAF to win the award. This was the third top unit win for the Hooligans, with the previous two occurring in 1970 and 1972, plus the top F-4 unit win in 1986. The Hooligans were also awarded the Hughes Trophy for the second time in 1994, twenty years after winning in 1974. The NDANG is to date the only Air National Guard squadron to have won the trophy twice and is the only F-16 squadron to have won it as well. Col. Lyle Andvik served as the fighter wing commander from 1999 until 2001, with Col. Richard Utecht commanding from 2001 to 2004. During the F-16 era, the Happy Hooligans maintained several alert detachments throughout the United States. The Hooligans had detachments at

Kingsley Field, Oregon; March Air Force Base (AFB), California; and Langley AFB, Virginia. The Kingsley Field alert detachment ended in 1994, but the March and Langley detachments lasted until the end of the fighter mission in 2007. The Langley detachment played a role in one of the darkest days in American history, when on September 11, 2001, hijacked airlines struck targets in New York City and Washington, DC, and a third was brought down in a Pennsylvanian farm field by its passengers. The 178th FS alert detachment at Langley scrambled several of its F-16s in an attempt to stop the airliners from reaching their intended targets, but unfortunately, it was too late. The Hooligans were the first USAF aircraft to reach the Pentagon that day and maintained continuous air cover over the city for more than 24 hours. Col. Robert Becklund became the last fighter-era commander from August 2004 until December 2009. He later became a brigadier general as the NDANG chief of staff for air, just as his father, Thornton Becklund, had done in 1993. The Happy Hooligans have always been innovators. "We were one of the first (if not the first) units to use night vision devices in the cockpit," said Becklund. "To do so, we had to modify the interior lighting to green since the instrument lighting was white, which interfered with the night vision devices (NVDs). Initially, we used green glow sticks in strategic places around the cockpit and then something we called Christmas tree lights (battery-operated green lights on a string strung around the cockpit)." In 2005, the Base Realignment and Closure Commission (BRAC) initially recommended that the NDANG be realigned with a move to the Grand Forks AFB and the mission of the NDANG be changed. Community leaders hired an independent evaluation firm to do a study, which, along with a formal hearing, may have contributed to the BRAC recommendation to leave the NDANG base in Fargo and convert it to the remotely piloted aircraft mission. In late 2006 and early 2007, the F-16s at Fargo were sent to the boneyard and replaced by MQ-1 Predator and, later, MQ-9 Reaper unmanned aerial vehicles. This brought an end to the 60-plus-year fighter mission in Fargo, North Dakota.

One

WORLD WAR II ORIGINS

As the US Army Air Forces were demobilized in 1945 and 1946 following World War II, inactivated unit designations were allotted and transferred to various state and territorial Air National Guard bureaus to reestablish them as ANG units. The 178th Fighter Squadron was assigned the lineage of the 392nd Fighter Squadron, which fell under the 367th Fighter Group. The 392nd was a distinguished unit in World War II. It flew the Lockheed P-38J Lightning initially and transitioned to the Republic P-47D Thunderbolt. In June 1944, during the Battle of Normandy following the D-Day landings, the 392nd destroyed five German convoys and about 100 tanks in a single day.

The leading ace of the 367th FG was Capt. Larry "Scrapper" Blumer, a native of Kindred, North Dakota, who became known as the "fastest ace in a day" when he shot down five German fighters in 15 minutes on August 25, 1944. The 392nd FS received two Presidential Unit Citations for two separate events during the war. The first was in the P-38J for bombing and strafing actions on August 25, 1944. The second was while flying the P-47D when the squadron attacked the headquarters of the German army's Oberbefehlshaber West (commander in chief west) on March 19, 1945. After the war, the squadron was disbanded at Seymour-Johnson Field, North Carolina, on November 7, 1945. During its combat tour, the squadron was credited with 39.5 air-to-air victories over enemy aircraft, the most of any of the squadrons in the 367th Fighter Group.

Scrapper Blumer, a Kindred, North Dakota, native, stands in front of his Lockheed P-38J Lightning *Scrapiron IV*. There were three previous *Scrapirons*, all of which were forced to crash land. Blumer led the 367th Fighter Group with six aerial victories in the European Theater. He earned the title "fastest ace in a day" when he shot down five German aircraft in the span of 15 minutes. Blumer went on to command the 393rd Fighter Squadron from November 10, 1944, until the end of his combat tour in mid-January 1945. He died of leukemia on October 23, 1997, in Springfield, Oregon. (National Archives.)

A P-38 Lightning of the 367th FG escorts a B-17 Flying Fortress to its target somewhere over occupied Europe in July 1944. During World War II, small escort fighters like the P-38 were nicknamed "Little Friends" by the bomber crews. It was the responsibility of the Little Friends to defend the bomber formations from German fighter attacks. The 367th FS flew both bomber escort and ground interdiction missions in the P-38 and later the P-47 Thunderbolt. (National Archives.)

The 367th FG, including the 392nd FS, transitioned from the P-38 to the Republic P-47 Thunderbolt (pictured) in early January 1945. Interestingly, 392nd FS pilots flew combat missions in the P-38 while also training to become proficient in the P-47. Using the Thunderbolt, the 367th FG was cited in a Belgium Army Order of the Day, earning the Belgian Fourragere. (National Archives.)

On August 25, the 392nd FS received its first Distinguished Unit Citation. The 392nd was part of a large attack group on several Luftwaffe airfields and had to fly through an intense flak barrage to attack them. The 392nd engaged more than 30 FW-190 fighters that had just taken off. Group claims were 25 enemy aircraft destroyed, one probably destroyed, and 17 damaged, against the loss of six aircraft. (National Archives.)

A P-38 Lightning flies a combat air patrol over the Normandy coast. The 392nd FS flew missions maintaining air cover over ships carrying invasion troops on D-Day and the next three days. P-38 units stationed in England were selected for these missions with the expectation that the distinctive silhouette of the Lightning would prevent potential friendly fire incidents by anti-aircraft gunners mistaking them for enemy fighters. (National Archives.)

Lt. Duane "Pappy" Larson of the 504th FS, 339th FG, stands next to a P-51D Mustang. Larson was stationed at RAF Fowlmere, England. He flew the P-51D on 68 combat missions in the European Theater. He was awarded six flying medals and the Distinguished Flying Cross. He went on to become the commander of the 178th Fighter-Interceptor Squadron and attained the rank of brigadier general before he retired in 1969.

Two

FOUNDATIONS
IN THE MUSTANG

On May 24, 1946, the wartime 392nd FS was allocated to the National Guard and redesignated as the 178th Fighter Squadron. It was organized at Hector Field on the north end of Fargo and was federally recognized on January 16, 1947. The first muster of airmen for the North Dakota Air National Guard was 44 airmen and 23 officers. The first aircraft assigned to the 178th were P-51D Mustangs (later designated F-51Ds), AT-6 Texan trainers, B-26 Invaders, and C-47 Skytrain Operational Support Aircraft (OSAs). The first role of the North Dakota ANG was continental air defense, meaning that NDANG Mustang pilots were trained to intercept Soviet long-range bombers that were believed would come over the North Pole and attack targets in the United States. The 178th FS was mobilized in March 1951 during the Korean War and was moved to Moody Air Force Base in Georgia. While there, it was assigned to the 146th Fighter-Bomber Group, Strategic Air Command. In November 1951, the 178th was moved to George AFB in California and reassigned to Tactical Air Command (TAC). In January 1953, the 178th was returned to North Dakota state control and reactivated in Fargo as a fighter-interceptor squadron. The F-51D Mustangs continued to fly with the NDANG until the fall of 1954, when the unit transitioned to the F-94A/B Starfire interceptor.

This is what Hector Field looked like in June 1945. Prior to the North Dakota ANG, there was the Hector Military Airport. The Hector MAP was a major destination for US Army Air Forces pilots and aircraft as they made cross-country flights. Interestingly, Hector was also the staging location for P-39 Airacobra fighter planes that were going to be ferried to the Soviet Union.

The first formation of the 178th Fighter Squadron stands at attention at the Avalon Ballroom in Fargo, North Dakota.

Brig. Gen. Herbert L. Edwards, the North Dakota adjutant general (left), and Lt. Col. Richard D. Neece, the first 178th Fighter Squadron commander (right), are credited with assembling and organizing the North Dakota Air National Guard

Lt. Col. Richard D. Neece, the 178th FS commander, flies the first NDANG sortie in an AT-6 Texan. The flight was the delivery of the aircraft type to Fargo on January 20, 1947.

In February 1947, the first fighter aircraft assigned to the 178th FS, a P-51D Mustang, was delivered to Fargo from Kelly Field, Texas. The NDANG flew the P-51D Mustang from inception in 1947 until 1954. The "P" in P-51 stood for "Pursuit" and was changed to "F" for "Fighter" in 1948.

Before the full ramp was completed at Hector Field, the F-51D Mustangs and other aircraft assigned to the 178th FS had to operate from the nearby grass fields. For many of the original pilots of the NDANG, these conditions were similar to what they experienced in Europe during World War II.

One of the first structures occupied by the NDANG was the base operations building, left over by the USAAF's presence at Hector Field during World War II. This was where pilots underwent briefings and debriefs and prepared for missions. Here, it is seen during one of the massive snow storms during the winter of 1948–1949.

Some of the first F-51D Mustangs assigned to the NDANG sit on a snowy flight line during the early winter of 1949. Despite the large snowdrifts, NDANG pilots were able to successfully fly sorties without many issues.

The first officers of the NDANG are pictured here. In the first year, the 178th built itself from a purely paper organization to an efficiently coordinated unit with 50 officers and 299 men. In helping this expansion, one aggressive airman, Warren Johnson, brought 50 candidates out to enlist. For this, Johnson was given a free trip to the Army-Navy football game as a reward.

Lt. Col. Richard Neece, the 178th FS commander, writes on a chalkboard as he describes aerial strategy with fellow NDANG pilots. This photograph shows what a routine preflight briefing looked like for the NDANG in the first couple of years of the unit's existence.

From left to right, Alan R. Ostby, Darrol G. Schroeder, Verne E. Plath, Warren Johnson, James R. Holman, and Fredrick W. Quam converse alongside an F-51D Mustang. Schroeder left the NDANG, went active duty, received his pilot's wings, and flew F-86 Sabres in Europe before returning to the NDANG and, eventually, the rank of major general. Quam retired as a chief master sergeant.

North Dakota and Minnesota ANG aircraft are on the ramp at what is believed to be Casper Airport in Wyoming in 1949. Casper Airport was where many fighter squadrons went for summer training camp. These camps allowed pilots and ground crews to train in realistic combat scenarios. Of interesting note is the presence of C-47 cargo planes and B-26 and B-25 bombers.

NDANG member Don Matson, center, is among a group talking on an AN/GRC-26 Army/Navy Ground Radio Equipment. Often, it was jokingly referred to as an "ANGRY-26," and was usually transported using a 2.5-ton cargo truck. The unit consisted of a transportable assembly of transmission equipment with the radio being used alone or simultaneously with teletype operation.

These 178th FS members are bundled up on the flight line with F-51D Mustang aircraft at the NDANG base in Fargo. The photograph was originally labelled "Cold Airmen."

The NDANG C-47 was named *Minnie H* after a steamboat from the 1800s that sailed on Devil's Lake, North Dakota. From left to right are Frank Bringham, manager of Devil's Lake Airport; Lt. Donald Jones, assistant operations manager for the 178th FS; Col. Richard Neece, 178th FS commanding officer; H.J. Naugle, the son of Minne Naugle, for whom the original steamboat was named; Brig. Gen. H.L. Edwards, the North Dakota adjutant general; Maj. Leroy Landom, the NDANG property manager; and Sgt. Robert Olwin, crew chief.

This was one of the five B-26 Invader bombers owned by the 178th FS during the early years of the NDANG. The B-26 was originally built as the A-26 during World War II. From 1948 until 1965, it was called the B-26 Invader by the USAF but has since been commonly referred to by its World War II designation. The NDANG's B-26s were used as high-speed executive transports and mock enemy bombers during training exercises.

Capt. Marley Swanson, an NDANG pilot and longtime physical education teacher at Ben Franklin Junior High School in Fargo, stands in the cockpit of a B-26 Invader medium bomber during a deployment to Camp Williams, Wisconsin, in 1950. Swanson flew the B-26 for the NDANG from 1947 to 1951.

NDANG members walk on steel runway matting between six-person tents during the first annual summer camp training period at Hector Field, Fargo, North Dakota. The camp started on June 13, 1948, and lasted two weeks until June 25. The steel matting was used because of the heavy rains, which created muddy conditions for the entire training period.

NDANG members practice their marksmanship at their first summer camp at Hector Field in June 1948. They are using the M1 Carbine, a World War II–era lightweight, semi-automatic weapon chambered in .30-caliber carbine.

Lt. George Gorman (left) explains his encounter with an unidentified flying object to Dan Oxley and Duane Lund. The "Gorman Dogfight" occurred on October 1, 1948, and involved Lieutenant Gorman allegedly spotting and chasing a flying saucer over Fargo. The Hector Field control tower also allegedly saw the object. The story became immensely popular all over the country and even had the Army send several UFO investigators to interview those involved.

This North American B-25 Mitchell medium bomber (tail No. 44-30489) was assigned to the NDANG from 1954 to 1958. It was used as an executive transport and for training exercises. On a few occasions, it played the role of an "enemy bomber" tasked with bombing Fargo. Many Air National Guard fighter squadrons were assigned B-25s in the early postwar period. What happened to this B-25 after its time with the NDANG is unknown.

The two C-47 aircraft of the NDANG were called up during Operation Haylift to help deliver supplies to farmers, families, and livestock stranded due to the massive snow storms during the winter of 1948 and 1949. The missions were flown out of Minot, where hay, mail, and other essential supplies were loaded into the cargo doors of the C-47s and pushed out in areas where they could be easily accessible by individuals or hungry cattle.

From left to right, Don Coleman, Dan Oxley, Maj. Donald Johnson, and Lt. Col. Richard Neece discuss flight operations at a blackboard during Operation Haylift. In February 1949, during a flight back to Fargo from Minot, Major Johnson was killed when his F-51D Mustang crashed shortly after takeoff in bad weather. This was the first fatal crash of an NDANG Mustang. Major Johnson had been appointed commander of the 178th FS in July 1948.

Maj. Donald Jones, the 178th FS commander, fourth from left, stands with the rest of the 178th FS Operation Haylift crew for a quick pre-mission photograph with one of the C-47 aircraft involved in the operation.

NDANG members prepare to toss a hay bale out of the door of a C-47 during Operation Haylift. Note the rope tied around the crewman in the leather jacket. This was a crude safety measure to help save the crewman if he happened to fall out of the aircraft while they were dropping the hay. How effective it would have been, if at all, is unknown.

This aerial photograph shows Hector Field around 1949. Many of the buildings to the right were originally built by the USAAF during World War II and were taken over by the NDANG in 1947. By the mid-1950s, most of those buildings were torn down and replaced with more long-term structures. The building labelled "New Construction" is the main NDANG hangar.

Thornton "Beck" Becklund smiles for the camera as he sits on an F-51D Mustang during the annual training summer camp at Casper, Wyoming, in 1949. Thornton enlisted in the NDANG in 1948 in the "radio shop" and went on to earn a commission and become a pilot with the 178th. He attained the rank of brigadier general in 1983 and served as the chief of staff for the ANG until he retired in 1989.

Pictured from left to right are Richard Neece, Tom Marking, and R. Marshall Johnson in front of a wrecked NDANG F-51D Mustang near Casper during the 1949 summer training camp. There were a few NDANG Mustangs that went down during the summer camp. Fortunately, none of the pilots were seriously hurt in any of them. At best, like Tom Marking pictured here, they were a bit shaken up. The F-51 pictured was repaired and currently still flies as N151AF.

NDANG ground crewmen perform a final oil check on an F-51D Mustang prior to a sortie during the 1949 Casper summer training camp. One can imagine how loud it must have been for the two ground crewmen who are just a few feet away from the massive Mustang propellers.

From left to right, May Minor, Art Breyer, Fred Quam, and Howard Stewart march in the Fargo Armed Forces Day Parade in downtown Fargo in May 1950. Breyer, a combat veteran of the 101st Airborne Division during World War II, always carried the flag when the color guard performed in special events. Once, prior to a performance, strong winds broke the flagpole and forced Breyer to hold it together as he marched.

Warren Sunde puts fuel into an NDANG pickup truck at the "motor pool" in the early 1950s. The motor pool, including this fueling station, was just off the old flight line and almost between the old hangar and the new one.

MOTOR POOL

NDAK ANG FARGO, NDAK

This is one of the first photographs of the NDANG Auger Inn all-ranks club during the early years of the unit's existence. The Auger Inn was originally in the old World War II dining hall, which was a wooden temporary building of the period. The west leg of the building held a bar, storage, and dining booths; the east leg was a dining area with tables that could be moved for dancing.

Pictured clockwise from Earl Anderson (in leather jacket) at the old Auger Inn are NDANG members Don Teigen, Don Matson, Merve Beynon, Gordy Gronland, Bob Olwin, Duane Campbell, Jim Winkler, Ed Shoonmaker, and Don Foster, described as an "elite" group.

During the Korean War, roughly 50 officers and 350 enlisted members of the NDANG were activated for duty. In addition to the men, eight North American F-51D Mustangs were sent to California to be refitted for ground attack missions before being sent overseas to South Korea. Two NDANG members were killed while training in the United States, and several more, including three officers, were killed while serving in Korea.

Members of the NDANG mount a High Velocity Aircraft Rocket (HVAR) to the underside of an F-51D Mustang during a training exercise at George AFB, California, in 1951. When the 178th was mobilized during the Korean War, many unit members were sent to George AFB to train for service overseas. Several of the unit's F-51Ds were also acquired and sent to Korea to fly in the air interdiction role.

NDANG members pass the time by playing cards in the barracks while based at Moody AFB, Georgia, in February 1951.

NDANG member Capt. Don Satran stands next to the K-6 Air Base Headquarters sign in Korea in April 1952. The K-6 base was near Pyeongtaek, which later became Camp Humphreys and then US Army Garrison-Humphreys (USAG-H).

Second Lt. Alexander Macdonald, right, stands next to a Jeep while serving in Korea. During the Korean War, he flew 36 combat sorties, all in the LT-6G, a forward observer variant of the T-6 Texan. On these combat sorties, an Army artillery observer flew in the back seat and did most of the radio communications with the infantrymen on the ground. The pilot flew the aircraft and talked to the fighters when they used them for close air support.

An LT-6G is in the skies over Korea during the war. These World War II–era training aircraft were modified for artillery spotting and close air support. They were nicknamed "mosquitos." Their job was often dangerous, as they lacked heavy armor plating and were easy targets for enemy anti-aircraft gunners.

From left to right, Capt. R. Marshall Johnson, Capt. Don Satrom, and Lt. Col. Wells pose in Korea in July 1952. Johnson and Satrom were some of the NDANG officers deployed for the Korean War. Johnson flew 60 combat missions during the war, most often firing smoke rockets from his LT-6G while flying behind enemy lines to mark locations for fighter-bombers to target.

Lt. William Christianson (left) and Lt. Russell Van Hellen review a map as they prepare to fly NDANG F-51Ds during Operation Longhorn in June 1952. Operation Longhorn was a training exercise that saw various ANG F-51 units, including the 178th FS stationed at George AFB, California, practice responding to a simulated aerial attack on Texas. The NDANG flew and operated from the now-closed James Connally AFB in Waco, Texas.

Maj. R. Marshall Johnson stands at the podium to speak during a welcome home ceremony in January 1953 for unit members activated for the Korean War. From left to right are Homer Goebel, Ed Stern, unidentified, Marsh Johnson (behind the microphone), Col. Herman Brocupp, North Dakota governor C. Norman Brunsdale, four unidentified, and Wilfred Housenga at far right.

Members of the 178th depart Fargo on their way to Camp Williams in Wisconsin for the annual summer training camp in June 1953. While the pilots and officers flew out in either the F-51Ds, B-26s, or the C-47s, the enlisted men had to take charter buses, trucks, and other USAF automobiles for the roughly 420 mile trip between Fargo and Camp Williams (now Volk Field).

All pilots were expected to attend the summer camps, including the veterans. World War II veteran Duane "Pappy" Larson goes over a preflight briefing at Camp Williams in Wisconsin in 1953. Pappy had an illustrious career with the 178th FS, attaining the rank of brigadier general before retiring in 1969.

S.Sgt. Everett Brust of the NDANG takes notes for an image caption while at Camp Williams during the summer training exercise in June 1953. Most of the images in this chapter were taken by Staff Sergeant Brust, who was the first photo lab chief with the NDANG. He retired from the NDANG in April 1987 after 40 years of service.

A staff sergeant rearms a North Dakota Air National Guard F-51D Mustang with .50-caliber bullets at Camp Williams, Wisconsin, in June 1953. The F-51D was armed with six .50-caliber machine guns with a total of 1,880 rounds. Four hundred rounds were in each inboard gun, and 270 in each outboard gun. The belt of bullets was nine yards long, which resulted in the saying, "Give them the whole nine yards."

NDANG pilot Bob Olwin listens to his crew chief while in the cockpit of his F-51D Mustang at Camp Williams in June 1953. The name of the crew chief is unknown.

A section from the 178th Fighter Squadron undergoes a basic training march at Camp Williams in June 1953.

Maj. Duane Larson, sixth from left, was one of the early NDANG leaders and a 178th Fighter Squadron commander in the mid-1960s. He later became a brigadier general. Because of his fatherly instincts, Larson became known as "Pappy" to his entire squadron. His men were dubbed "Hooligans" for their mischievous off-duty antics. Locally, they became known as "Pappy and his Hooligans." Because of Pappy's striking resemblance to a comic strip character of the day named Happy Easter, the squadron was soon known as "Happy and his Hooligans," later shortened to "the Happy Hooligans." The Happy Hooligans became the official nickname in the 1960s and was used as a tail flash (below) for the first time in 1964 on an F-89J aircraft.

From left to right, NDANG pilots Orin Stenehjem, Tom Stewart, Jim Greene, and Ken Schulstad pose wearing early overwater gear. NDANG pilots did not fly wearing this type of gear very often. It was usually worn when flying to the 179th FS at Minnesota ANG in Duluth.

From left to right, NDANG F-51 mechanics Fred Quam, Glenn Philbrick, and Gordon Wilde work on an NDANG Mustang sometime in the early 1950s. Quam was a Fargo native and mechanic of B-25s and A-26s during World War II. He returned to Fargo after the war and was one of the original members of the NDANG in 1947. As of 2022, he was the last surviving member of the original NDANG first muster.

Members of the 178th Maintenance Squadron sight and rearm the guns of F-51D Mustang No. 44-75009 in the NDANG's old hangar. Sighting the guns was a vital task, as without it, the plane's guns would not be accurate. This F-51D is still flying today with the name *Rosalie* and the FAA number N51TC.

View of the old ND Air National Guard ramp, circa 1954.
From left to right: a B-25 "Mitchell" bomber, two AT-6's, and six F-51D "Mustangs". Next to the hangar is a C-47 Transport and a P2V "Neptune"

The ramp at Hector Field is pictured during the F-51D Mustang era of the NDANG. In addition to the usual NDANG mission aircraft, there is an Aeronca L-16 belonging to the Civil Air Patrol and a Stinson Reliant Gull-Wing on the ramp as well. Furthermore, tucked in the far right corner behind the C-47 is the cockpit section of a Naval Air Station Minneapolis-based P2V Neptune.

Three

THE NDANG
ENTERS THE JET AGE

In early November 1954, the 178th FIS started the transition from the propeller-driven F-51D Mustang to the Lockheed F-94 Starfire. The F-94 was equipped with a 20mm cannon and a radar in the nose. The North Dakota Air National Guard was one of the few units to fly all three variants of the F-94 Starfire, receiving the penultimate version, the F-94C Starfire, in 1957. During the F-94 era, the NDANG was also allowed to expand to the group level. On April 15, 1956, the 178th expanded to become the 119th Fighter Group (air defense) and had the 178th as the flying unit with other, non-flying squadrons being designated with the 119th. Despite the F-94's relatively short service life, the NDANG put it to good use as it maintained constant alert readiness in the event that they were needed to intercept a Soviet bomber threat.

An NDANG F-51D Mustang taxis by its eventual successor; the Lockheed F-94B. This photograph was taken in the latter part of 1954, shortly before the F-94s completely replaced the Mustangs. This F-94 is actually a Lockheed YF-94, tail No. 48-373. This was the second aircraft built from a Lockheed TF-80C. It was probably in Fargo for a familiarization visit to give pilots and ground crew an idea of their next mission aircraft.

The last NDANG F-51D Mustang (serial No. 44-72966) prepares to depart Hector Field in April 1954 with its newly-arrived successor in the background. Many of the early F-94A/Bs delivered to the NDANG came from the active duty 64th, 65th, and 66th Fighter-Interceptor Squadrons stationed at Elmendorf AFB in Alaska. The F-94B in the background (serial No. 50-936) was last assigned to the 66th Fighter-Interceptor Squadron.

The NDANG base at Hector Field is pictured around the early 1950s. The "new hangar," which today is the main hangar, had just completed construction around this time. Note the airplane seemingly in the middle of a field. That is an F-51D Mustang, tail No. 44-74407, which was preserved as a "gate guard." Today, this Mustang is on display in the Heritage Park on base.

A USAF aircraft marshaller brings in a 178th FIS F-94B to rest. The structure in the background was the main hangar at Casper Airfield in Wyoming. Also of note is the North American F-86 Sabre in the background, partially blocked by the marshaller. It is still common during training exercises for aircraft and personnel of different units to operate alongside one another for training and familiarization.

Two NDANG maintenance personnel are working on an ejection seat for one of the unit's F-94Bs. When they were packed in tight as seen here, most of the 178th FIS's F-94s could be kept inside and out of the elements.

This photograph shows Operational Support Aircraft (OSAs) that were flown by the North Dakota ANG in 1956. From left to right are a North American B-25 Mitchell, a Beech C-45 Expeditor, and a Douglas C-47 Skytrain. All three of these aircraft were used in a variety of roles, most notably as executive transport for high-ranking members of the unit, and in the case of the C-47, transporting the governor of North Dakota and his family.

NDANG member Senior Airman Norman Kenney pumps oxygen into the onboard oxygen tanks lin an F-94B while another airman monitors the amount being pumped in from the cockpit.

This photograph, taken sometime in late fall 1955, shows members of the NDANG outside the iconic Fargo Theater in downtown Fargo. According to the caption on the original photograph, the men had just enjoyed a viewing of an official unit film. Which film that was is sadly unknown.

Pilot Ardel Ness (left) and radar operator Harry Lohse enter the cockpit of a Lockheed F-94B. The 178th FIS was one of the few ANG interceptor squadrons that flew all three variants of the F-94.

The differences between the F-94A/B and F-94C variants of Starfire can clearly be seen here. While the F-94A/Bs had machine guns mounted in the nose, the F-94C had the guns removed and replaced with all-rocket armament consisting of four groups of six rockets in a ring around the nose. There was also the option to have rockets fitted in pods on both the wings and on hard points underneath the wings.

Brig. Gen. Winston P. Wilson, chief of the Air Force Division, National Guard Bureau, Washington, DC (right), presents the NDANG's first Air Force Flying Safety Award for July 1, 1954, to December 31, 1954, to Col. R. Marshall Johnson, 178th FIS commander, on April 12, 1955. Johnson was the 178th FS commander from 1951 to 1956 and the 119th FG commander from 1958 to 1968.

Col. Homer Goebel accepts a plaque reading "Air Defense Command" from an unidentified lieutenant general. The NDANG became an active member of the US defense structure when it began its 14-hour Air Defense Command alert missions in August 1954. Goebel was the first 119th Fighter Group commander in 1956 and "base technician" commander until 1968. He also became the first NDANG general officer in 1963.

An NDANG member loads a Mk. 4 folding-fin aerial rocket (FFAR, also sometimes referred to as a "Mighty Mouse") onto an F-94C Starfire in the 1950s. The Mighty Mouse was a 2.75-inch unguided rocket that was intended to be fired into large enemy bomber formations. The rocket's accuracy was relatively poor because its speed and spin rate were too low to effectively counter gravity drop, crosswinds, and dispersion.

Maj. R. Marsh Johnson (left) explains the use of the Del Mar aerial reflective target to Colonel Riddle. The target was towed behind a T-33 aircraft to train pilots in detecting and tracking aerial targets and the use of various automatic equipment for such purposes as fire control, missile launch control, and target interception. The tow target carried an electronic transmitter-receiver unit, which functioned as a miss-distance indicator to transmit information by radio.

Maj. R. Marsh Johnson, the 119th FG commander (far right), shakes hands with Lt. Richard Lucas, radar observer, as Capt. Pappy Larson emerges from the cockpit of an NDANG F-94C Starfire in April 1957. Larson and Lucas were the first Air National Guard aircrew to become combat qualified in an all-weather rocket-firing aircraft.

From left to right, R. Marsh Johnson, Richard Lucas, and Duane "Pappy" Larson examine wing camera footage from an F-94C Starfire. They are looking for any possible hits on a Del Mar target from the Grand Marais range.

From left to right, Donald Flesland, Alexander Macdonald, R. Marsh Johnson, Thor Hertsgaard, and Duane Larson discuss the handling of the F-94C Starfire.

Wayne Solberg stands next to an F-94 on the flight line of the NDANG in 1955. Solberg was well known for shooting down a drone target while flying an F-102 on deployment to Tyndall AFB, Florida, in 1966 and eventually became an NDANG brigadier general. He is the patriarch of a long line of Happy Hooligans, with all six of his children and eight grandchildren serving in the NDANG at some point.

First Lt. Alexander Macdonald (left) and 2nd Lt. Donald Flesland pose alongside an NDANG F-94C Starfire in the 1950s. Macdonald commanded the 119th Fighter Group from February 1968 to September 1974, and again from December 1974 to February 1981. Flesland reached the rank of lieutenant colonel and took command of the 178th FIS in 1968.

This photograph of 178th FIS personnel is believed to have been taken at Camp Williams, Wisconsin, in the late 1950s. Camp Williams was renamed Volk Field in honor of 1st Lt. Jerome A. Volk, the first Wisconsin ANG pilot killed in combat during the Korean War.

Airman 1st Class Erlyn Carlson's 1952 Mercury two-door hardtop is parked in front of an NDANG F-94C Starfire at the base in Fargo in October 1956. Carlson and seven other members of the "Toppers" car club brought the car to Minneapolis to enter it in the Gopher State Timing Association Custom and Hot Rod show. The group won several awards, including the most popular custom.

Capt. Robert Farris, 178th FIS operations officer (far right), briefs pilots and radar operators on a rocket mission at the NDANG base during the F-94C era. From left to right are (kneeling) 1st Lt. Jack Delvo, 1st Lt. Les Smith, and 2nd Lt. Neil Modin; (standing) 2nd Lt. Harry Lohse, 2nd Lt. Jim Powers, Capt. Robert Olwin, 1st Lt. William Harkins, and Capt. Duane Larson.

The NDANG operated a Beech C-45H Expeditor for a brief time from 1955 to 1959. The Expeditor served as a utility transport and supported the North Dakota National Guard state headquarters staff. The C-45 is a 6–11 passenger twin-engine, low-wing, conventional-gear aircraft. The C-45H pictured here was given to the North Dakota Highway Department in 1959. It survives today at the Beechcraft Heritage Museum in Tullahoma, Tennessee.

Senior Airman Al Hoff helps direct traffic at the intersection of Eleventh Street North and Twelfth Avenue North in front of Prairie Lutheran Church in North Fargo. The F5 tornado that hit Fargo on June 20, 1957, passed through many North Fargo neighborhoods and killed 12 people. It remains the deadliest tornado in North Dakota history.

NDANG member Frank Bourdon helps direct traffic in front of the wreckage of what is believed to be the old Fargo Central High School.

North Dakota governor John E. Davis, in a dark suit and tie, walks with NDANG leaders as he arrives at Volk Field, Wisconsin. Governor Davis was the first North Dakota governor to ride in an NDANG fighter jet. Note the tail of the NDANG's famed C-47 *Minnie H* in the background. In addition to serving the NDANG, *Minnie H* was also the personal transport plane of the North Dakota governor from 1947 to 1969.

The NDANG held an annual Christmas party and banquet, like this one, in the hangar each December from at least 1951 through 1959.

Santa Claus has been making an appearance at the Auger Inn all-ranks club for the children's party for many years. Here, Santa is seen making a grand entrance with NDANG pilots Basil Walker and Bob Farris sometime during the F-94B era.

From left to right, Airman 3rd Class Bill Lorenz, Staff Sgt. Merlin Gross, and Airman 1st Class Bill Kruger hang out on the left wing of an NDANG T-33 Shooting Star at Volk Field, Wisconsin, during one of the unit's summer camp training sessions.

Radar operators of the 178th FIS Lt. Earl "Shell" Gordon (left) and Lt. Roger Gurley pose for a lighthearted photograph in 1959. This image was sent out to other Air Defense Command squadrons on the 178th FIS Christmas card.

Four

NDANG Becomes Nuclear Capable

Starting in 1960, the 178th FIS was the first Air National Guard interceptor unit to serve on nuclear alert. When the F-94C Starfires were retired in 1959, the NDANG received the Northrop F-89 Scorpion. Like the F-94, the F-89 was a two-seat interceptor that featured rocket pods for intercepting large formations of enemy bombers. The F-89 may have been a bit slower than the previous F-94, but it made up for its lack of speed with its armament. The F-89 was the first aircraft capable of firing the first air-to-air nuclear rocket, the AIR-2 Genie. In addition to the two AIR-2 Genies, another version of the F-89 could fire 52 individual Mighty Mouse rockets in two separate wingtip pods. While flying the F-89, the NDANG attended the annual Ricks Trophy competition in August 1964 at Tyndall AFB, Florida. The 178th came in second place during the event with the weapons loader taking home the "Top Honor" trophy. The F-89 was also the first NDANG fighter aircraft to fly with the now world-famous "Happy Hooligans" nickname written on it. In 1965, the NDANG was recognized as the best of all flying units under Air Defense Command. The F-89s were eventually phased out in 1966, with the NDANG being one of the last squadrons to fly the type.

The NDANG received its first Northrop F-89 Scorpions in early 1959, with the unit becoming combat-ready the following year. The initial Scorpions delivered to the 178th were the F-89D variants. These models featured rocket pods mounted on the outside wing tanks. These were eventually removed in favor of adding fuel tanks with the F-89J variant.

Maj. Pappy Larson talks on a telephone receiver from the new battle control center (BCC) as Maj. Robert Farris and Lt. Roger Gurley look on in November 1960. The new BCC was considered one of the most important improvements in preparation for an annual operational readiness inspection for the 119th Fighter-Interceptor Group.

NDANG F-89J aircrew pose in March 1961. From left to right are 1st Lt. Wallace Frederickson, Capt. Donald Flesland, Lt. Col. Pappy Larson, Maj. Alexander Macdonald, and Capt. Harry Lohse Jr. These 178th FIS members were recognized with the "Expert Award," which is the highest rating awarded to pilots and radar observers by Air Defense Command. These members were the first of 40 ANG units under ADC to qualify for the award.

Members of the 178th FIS run to their F-89J Scorpion aircraft as they scramble during an operational readiness check at the North Dakota ANG base in Fargo in March 1960.

From left to right, Floyd Broadland, Bill Nolte, Gordon Wilde, and Al Huff stand in front of an F-89 being worked on in the early 1960s. Wilde was killed in January 1963 when he was drawn into the intake of an F-89 during a maintenance test. Broadland was one of four NDANG members killed in the 1969 C-54 crash during the Alaska deployment.

A USAF Kaman HH-43B Huskie rescue helicopter hoists an NDANG pilot out of Pelican Lake near Pelican Rapids, Minnesota. This was during the July 1963 air rescue training session done in conjunction with a rescue squadron from Minot AFB, North Dakota. The HH-43B pictured here, tail No. 60-0280, was one of the two assigned to Minot AFB and was eventually sent to Vietnam in August 1964.

Maj. Alexander Macdonald stands on the platform, as Darrol Schroeder (holding helmet), Duane Nagle (with glasses on left), and Bill Hawkins (at right side behind the "dunker") are among the Happy Hooligans participating in pilot rescue training at Pelican Lake on July 27, 1963. This aerial recovery training was designed to help NDANG aircrews prepare and train for recovery in the event that they had to eject from their aircraft over water.

NDANG pilot Lt. Col. James A. Peterson winces at the moment of impact with Pelican Lake during 1963 air rescue training.

Col. R. Marsh Johnson, 119th Group commander (upper left) directs the defense condition under fallout DECUF operation from the command post during the March 1964 unit training assembly at the NDANG. From left to right facing the camera are Lt. Col. Marley Swanson, Maj. G.M. Kroeber, and Lt. Col. Thomas Marking. The ability to conduct basic operations of the NDANG after a nearby nuclear explosion and resultant fallout was tested and verified.

Tech. Sgt. Jack Tietgens (right) checks the identification card of Lt. Kenneth Haugen in April 1964. Haugen, a longtime North Dakota and Minnesota resident, went on to become the director of flight operations at the National Aeronautics and Space Administration (NASA).

An NDANG F-89J Scorpion crew prepares to deliver human blood during a mercy flight in the mid-1960s. NDANG mercy flights were common, using both personnel and cargo transport aircraft as well as fighters when speed was necessary.

NDANG members pose as they prepare to go to Tyndall AFB, Florida, to compete in the annual Ricks Trophy competition in the fall of 1964. The 178th FIS competed against eight other ANG interceptor squadrons flying similar aircraft. The contest was designed to test the capability of air and ground crews in combat scenarios.

A 178th FIS, 119th FIG F-89J Scorpion is pictured in flight over North Dakota. The F-89J was capable of carrying the AIR-2 Genie, an air-to-air nuclear rocket designed to be fired into large Soviet bomber formations to take out as many aircraft as possible in the blast radius of roughly 1,000 feet.

This photograph, facing east along Nineteenth Avenue in North Fargo, catches an NDANG F-89J taking off from Hector Field heading south in the mid-1960s. The F-89, while maybe not the best-looking or fastest jet flown by the NDANG, holds a special place in the history of the unit as it was the first aircraft to carry the world-famous nickname "the Happy Hooligans."

Five

THE HOOLIGANS
GO SUPERSONIC

In September 1966, the 178th FIS received its first F-102A Delta Daggers. The F-102A was the USAF's first operational supersonic interceptor and delta-wing fighter. It used an internal weapons bay to carry both guided missiles and rockets. It was the first time since the F-51 Mustang that the NDANG flew a single-seat interceptor, although the TF-102A was a side-by-side dual trainer version of the F-102 that was also flown by the 178th. In 1968, the NDANG was the only Air National Guard unit to receive the flying safety award. It was the second one awarded to the 178th FIS, with the first being issued in 1959. During the three-year span of F-102s, the NDANG retired its longtime workhorse VC-47 *Minnie H*, and in its place came the C-54 Skymaster. One of those Skymasters was lost during the 178th's 1969 deployment to Alaska on August 27, 1969. Onboard the flight was Lt. Col. Donald H. Flesland, Capt. Eddie E. Stewart, Master Sgt. Floyd D. Broadland, and Master Sgt. Ingvald Nelson. Lieutenant Colonel Flesland was the commander of the 178th FIS at the time of the accident. In 1969, the 178th FIS replaced its F-102s with F-101Bs, with many of the latter being sent to other F-102 Air National Guard units or the boneyard in Arizona.

The Happy Hooligans received their first Convair F-102A Delta Dagger in July 1966; however, the rest of the fleet did not arrive until the fall of that year. The "Deuces," as they were commonly nicknamed, replaced the F-89 Scorpions that the unit had been flying since May 1958.

Chief Master Sgt. Ray Skramstad talks on the maintenance control radio at the NDANG base in 1966. The radio was used to communicate with ground maintenance personnel on the flight line as well as pilots in the aircraft. Of interesting note is the aircraft locator chart in the background. This told the controller the status of all 178th FIS interceptor aircraft. It also features a diagram of the layout of Hector Airport at bottom right.

A Happy Hooligan F-102A Delta Dagger sits in an "alert barn" at the NDANG base. Pilots were standing by 24 hours a day, seven days a week, ready to hop into the cockpit in response to Cold War threats.

NDANG weapons loaders, including Airman 1st Class William Gilge (center), load an AIM-4 air-to-air missile onto an F-102A Delta Dagger in the late 1960s.

The missing propeller of the 119th Wing's C-54 Skymaster is lifted out of the Illinois farm field it landed in after coming loose in-flight on November 18, 1967. At the time of the incident, the Skymaster was being flown by Lt. Col. Alexander Macdonald and Lt. Col. Thornton "Beck" Becklund. Among the high-profile passengers were North Dakota governor Bill Guy and his wife. Macdonald and Becklund successfully landed the Skymaster with no serious problems.

The NDANG Douglas C-54 Skymaster sits on the ramp at Chanute AFB, Illinois, with its No. 3 engine missing. During the landing procedure, it was determined that the propeller had damaged the right side landing gear when it separated from the aircraft. Macdonald and Becklund had to circle Chanute AFB while the aircrew manually lowered the damaged landing gear. The plane landed with no difficulties.

The NDANG side of Hector Field is seen from the air in the late 1960s. Most, if not all, of the 178th FIS's F-102s can be seen on the ramp by the newer hangar. The old hangar, at left, has three of the squadron's T-33s lined up, plus the C-47 *Minnie H.*

Capt. Jerome Fischer, 178th FIS pilot, executed an F-102 "nose wheel up landing" at the NDANG base on March 7, 1968. The malfunction was caused when a compass amplifier came loose in the nose wheel well and lodged the gear in the up formation. The F-102 was repaired and returned to service.

F-102A Delta Dagger (tail No. 56-1480) undergoes maintenance on a snow-covered NDANG base flight line in the late 1960s. The new, larger hangar could only fit so many F-102s, so a few had to remain on the flight line even in the most extreme weather. Tail No. 56-1480 was eventually converted to a PQM-102 target drone and was shot down in November 1975.

Col. Marsh Johnson, the 119th Fighter Group commander, right, climbs into a Convair TF-102 Delta Dagger aircraft with an unidentified rider at the NDANG base, probably in 1966. The TF-102A differed from the F-102 because it had a wider forward fuselage so it could seat two crew members side-by-side for training.

A patient is loaded onto *Minnie H* during one of her several mercy flights. During these flights, NDANG flight surgeon Lt. Col. Duane Nagle and his medical service assistants, S.Sgt. Ronald Helgeson and Airman 1st Class Larry Gronland, would help care for the patients until they reached their destination

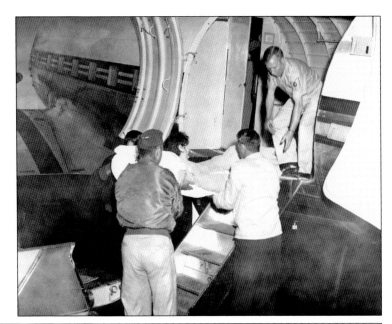

To Col. Larson — on her last day!
1-30-68 Bill Guy, Gov. N.D.

This is an autographed photograph from North Dakota governor Bill Guy to Lt. Col. Pappy Larson from *Minnie H*'s final flight from Fargo to Bismarck on January 30, 1968. From left to right are Master Sgt. Ingvald Nelson, who served as the flight engineer and crew chief for most of the 20 years that *Minnie H* was in North Dakota; Capt. Dennis Dietzler; Lt. Col. Pappy Larson; Lt. Col. Alexander Macdonald; Governor Guy; North Dakota adjutant general Maj. Gen. LaClair Melhouse; Col. R. Marsh Johnson; Lt. Col. Thornton "Beck" Becklund; and Tech. Sgt. Dale Ness.

After her retirement, *Minnie H* sat outside at the State Historical Museum in Bismarck for five years before having her wings removed and a shed built around her. In 1988, she was transported via an Army National Guard CH-54 Skycrane and placed on display at Bonanzaville's Eagles Air Museum in West Fargo, North Dakota. This is how she looks today. (Photograph by Maxwell Sabin.)

Brig. Gen. I.G. Brown, assistant chief for the ANG in Washington, DC (left), presents the Flying Safety Award to Col. Alexander P. Macdonald, the 119th FIG commander. The NDANG achieved the second USAF flying safety award in its history, with the first being in 1959. The 178th FIS compiled 5,709 accident-free flying hours in the 1968 calendar year in the F-102A and T-33.

This is the official patch of the 119th FIG. The bar in the center is symbolic of sky and clouds, the elements of aviation. The arrows illustrate the unit's motto, "Guarding the Northland." The central arrow points to the north with two crossed arrows, while the shield suggests military security. The gold and green of the background allude to the Dakota farmlands and grains produced there. The patch also uses the USAF colors golden yellow and ultramarine blue.

The NDANG received its first C-54 Skymaster in April 1967 to supplement, and eventually replace, the beloved C-47 *Minnie H.* On August 27, 1969, the C-54 vanished over Alaska during a flight from Elmendorf AFB to King Salmon Air Force Station. Onboard the plane at the time was pilot and 178th FIS commander Lt. Col. Donald H. Flesland, co-pilot Capt. Eddie E. Stewart, flight chief Master Sgt. Floyd D. Broadland, and crew chief Master Sgt. Ingvald Nelson. The wreckage was not found until August 30, 1972, almost three years later. There were no survivors.

NDANG members work on repair and updates to a memorial at Camp Carroll, Alaska, in early September 1969. The memorial was dedicated to the four NDANG members who were lost in the C-54 crash the previous month. The bricks used in the memorial were donated by the Hebron Brick Company of Hebron, North Dakota.

NDANG members train for domestic disturbance scenarios in downtown Fargo in 1967. Training like this was put to use when members of the North Dakota National Guard were activated in response to nearly 3,000 drunken college students who descended on the small town of Zap, North Dakota, in May 1969. What started as a North Dakota State University (NDSU) *Spectrum* newspaper joke became a serious overwhelming of the town by the students in what became known as "the Zip to Zap." Students were dispersed by North Dakota National Guard members with little resistance, and peace was restored.

Six

THE ONE-OH-WONDER ARRIVES IN FARGO

In 1969, the 178th FIS received its first F-101B Voodoos. The 178th was one of the first four ANG interceptor units to receive the Voodoo, with many of the aircraft coming from the recently deactivated 18th FIS at Grand Forks AFB. Not long after the F-101Bs arrived in Fargo, their pilots and crews were put to the test during the 1970 USAF Weapons Competition, also known as William Tell. Not only did the Hooligans come in first for the F-101B category, but Capt. James Reimers and Capt. Arthur Jacobson were awarded the Top Gun trophy for being the best aircrew in the entire competition. This was no small feat considering their competition was fellow Air National Guardsmen, active duty personnel, and Royal Canadian Air Force crews. The following year, the 178th won the Winston P. Wilson and the Distinguished Flying Unit Award. The NDANG began its string of flying safety with 20,860.4 hours and 13,907 sorties without a class-A mishap in the F-101.

NDANG weapon loaders practice loading an inert AIR-2 Genie rocket onto a newly arrived McDonnell F-101B Voodoo fighter-interceptor. In the background behind the load team is one of the NDANG's F-102s that had recently been replaced.

NDANG members display awards at the 1970 William Tell air-to-air fighter competition at Tyndall AFB, Florida, in October 1970. From left to right are Capt. James Reimers, Capt. Arthur Jacobson, Lt. Col. Wally Hegg, Maj. Allan Eide, and Col. Alexander Macdonald. Captains Reimers and Jacobson were voted the top aircrew at the competition. This is no small feat considering they had just started flying the F-101B the previous year and were competing against other ANG, active duty, and Canadian pilots and ground crews.

Pictured are members of the 1970 NDANG first-place William Tell weapons load team. From left to right are Sgt. William Gilge, Staff Sgt. Merlyn Dorrheim and Staff Sgt. Kenneth Smallarz. The team coach (not pictured) was Master Sgt. James Schreiner, and the reserve member of the team was Staff Sgt. Phillip Poe. The weapons load team was graded in its ability to properly load and arm an F-101B Voodoo aircraft with different types of ordnance.

Airman Pam Miller (left) and Airman Paula Toay stand near an NDANG F-101B in the early 1970s. They enlisted as part of the Women's Air Force (WAF) program, with early roles for females being limited to mostly administrative duties. Toay was the first woman to enlist in the WAF program at the NDANG in June 1971.

NDANG pilot 1st Lt. Burton Humphrey was killed on March 23, 1972, when his F-101B Voodoo crashed a mile and a half south of Hector Airport. The F-101B crashed after takeoff when Humphrey and WSO 2nd Lt. Sanford Borlaug could not get sufficient altitude on takeoff into prevailing winds and were forced to eject. The two stayed with the jet long enough to make sure it would not crash into a residential neighborhood. Borlaug survived the crash with only a broken arm and multiple bruises.

Tech. Sgt. Loren Bergerson secures 1st Lt. Ron Saeger into the back seat of an F-101B Voodoo. In 1971, the NDANG was selected for the Winston P. Wilson trophy over 54 other ANG squadrons that served as either fighter, fighter-interceptor, or reconnaissance squadrons.

An NDANG F-101B fires an AIM-4 Falcon heat-seeking missile during a training exercise. In 1971, the NDANG won a Distinguished Flying Unit Award, one of five in the entire Air National Guard to receive such an honor.

This 1953 Convair VT-29B being refueled on the flight line of the NDANG replaced the NDANG's C-54 Skymaster as the unit's transport plane in May 1972. The VT-29B was somewhat smaller than the C-54, with a capacity of 17 passengers, but had greater fuel capacity and was pressurized. The NDANG flew two different VT-29s. A second twin-engine VT-29D arrived in May 1973.

The 178th FIS's 1972 William Tell aircrew team is seen here. From left to right are (first row) Capt. Thomas Polkinghorn, 1st Lt. Roger Olsen, 1st Lt. Terry Thilmony, Lt. Col. William Phelan, and 1st Lt. Steve Brosowke; (second row) Maj. Wally Hegg, Capt. John Foyen, Capt. Gary Kaiser, Capt. Douglas Macdonald, and Capt. Robert Carlson.

On March 17, 1973, two NDANG F-101B Voodoos had a mid-air collision over Fessenden, North Dakota. The crew of this F-101B was able to fly back to Fargo; however, the crew of the other F-101 was forced to eject. The F-101 crashed in an empty farm field a mile east and three miles south of Fessenden and was destroyed on impact. No one was seriously hurt during the accident. The F-101B that returned to base, tail No. 58-0341, was written off and is now on display in the Heritage Park at the NDANG base.

Maj. Gen. Lawrence Fleming, commander of the 24th NORAD Air Division at Malmstrom AFB, Montana, address the NDANG during awards ceremonies held on June 2, 1973. Standing from left to right are Tech. Sgt. Ron Larson, 1st Lt. Richard Crockett, Col. D.G. Schroeder, Col. A.P. Macdonald, and Maj. Gen. L.A. Melhouse.

Major Generals Fleming (left) and Melhouse, North Dakota adjutant general, stand next to an NDANG F-101B Voodoo with the first Air Force Outstanding Unit Award (AFOUA) ribbon to be placed on the tail of a Happy Hooligan F-101. The ribbon could only be seen on aircraft and NDANG personnel uniforms without any devices for the following two years, when it received its second AFOUA in 1975 for the period of July 1, 1972, through December 31, 1973.

The NDANG 1974 William Tell maintenance team is lined up with F-101B Voodoo tail No. 57-0297 in the background.

NDANG members hold the 1974 F-101 category William Tell Top Gun award, which was given to the best aircrew–maintenance team combination. From left to right are 1st Lt. Roger Hanson, WSO; Tech. Sgt. Richard McGuire, crew chief; Tech. Sgt. Armin Ding, radar specialist; and 1st Lt. William Dittmer, pilot.

Col. Thornton Becklund (left) and Col. Alexander Macdonald (right) are with the Hughes Trophy during a celebration following the formal unit recognition ceremony on December 7, 1974. The Hughes Trophy was given to the best air defense unit in the entire US Air Force.

From left to right, Lt. Col. Wally Hegg, Col. Alexander Macdonald, and Maj. Gen. William S. Harrell put the "A" award on the tail of an NDANG F-101B Voodoo. The A award was given for outstanding performance of the air defense mission. The NDANG won three A awards throughout the 1970s.

NDANG members, from right to left, Col. Thornton Becklund, chief of maintenance; Chief Master Sergeant Chester Nelson; and Senior Master Sgt. Christie Bark accept the 1974 Daedalion Maintenance Trophy during a ceremony with Gen. George S. Brown, commander of the US Air Force Systems Command at Andrews AFB, Maryland. Brown went on to become chairman of the Joint Chiefs of Staff.

Lt. Col. James Peterson (left) and Lt. Col. Leroy Aafedt (work in the safety office in the main hangar at the NDANG base. Sadly, both were killed in a T-33 accident near Northwood, North Dakota, on May 25, 1975. They were described as two of the unit's most capable and dedicated officers. At the time of the crash, Aafedt had recently been promoted to director of operations for the 119th FIG and Peterson was one of the Hooligans' two deputy commanders.

Senior Master Sgt. Duane Hinsperger works on the engine of an F-101 aircraft at the NDANG base sometime during the F-101B era of the Happy Hooligans. Hinsperger was a native of Jamestown, North Dakota, and joined the NDANG in 1952. He served with the Happy Hooligans for 38 years before retiring in 1990.

Second Lt. Marilyn (Koon) Mosser stands with Lt. Col. Ted Labernick, the NDANG Air Force adviser, following a T-33 orientation flight. In October 1976, Koon became the first woman ever selected from any of the nation's 91 Air Guard units for pilot training. She was a native of Beach, North Dakota, and an executive officer in the 178th FIS when she was selected. She was unable to fly fighter aircraft due to USAF rules at the time, so she transferred to the Arizona ANG's 161st ARG and flew KC-135 Stratotankers there. She was one of the pilots who flew on the first all-female aerial refueling flight in 1984.

Members of the first all-female weapons load team, from left to right, Sgt. Patricia McMerty, Airman 1st Class Jacqueline Sanders, Sgt. Ellen Rising, and Airman 1st Class Doreen Thomas load an inert AIR-2 Genie on an F-101 as inspectors watch with a critical eye for scoring at the William Tell air-to-air fighter competition at Tyndall AFB in October 1975.

McDonnell F-101B Voodoo No. 57-0417 comes in for a landing at Fargo Air National Guard base. Interestingly, this F-101 has been adorned with a lobster "zap," or graffiti. The lobster zap was the handiwork of the "Mainieacs" of the Maine Air National Guard who were known to be the tricksters of the Air National Guard, a tradition that continues today. The F-101B pictured here is currently on display in Florida.

Maj. Gen. John T. Guice, director of the Air National Guard (left) presents the National Guard Association of the US Distinguished Flying Unit Award to Col. Alexander Macdonald during a conference in New Orleans, Louisiana, on September 12, 1977.

Members of the 119th Civil Engineer Squadron, including Staff Sgt. John Carney, Airman Veril Larson, and Master Sgt. Fred Kaufman, pour concrete for an aircraft arresting system on the runway of Hector Field in Fargo in 1977 as a Northwest Orient 727 prepares to land. The aircraft arresting system used a cable across the runway that could be raised to catch the tailhook of an F-4 aircraft for controlled deceleration if there were braking problems during an aborted take-off or landing. It was needed because of the unit mission transition from the F-101 to the F-4.

Members of the 119th Aircraft Maintenance Unit Gordon Brekken (right) and Oscar Hanson load an aircraft deceleration parachute in the tail of an F-101 Voodoo as Chief Master Sgt. Fred Quam observes, at the NDANG base. The parachute was used to slow the aircraft upon landing.

A tail-chute is deployed for landing as an F-101 Voodoo lands at NDANG. The parachute was necessary to slow the aircraft for landing.

Seven

THE NORTHERN PLAINS RHINOS

In 1977, the NDANG received its first McDonnell F-4D Phantom IIs. Most, if not all, of the F-4s that it received had spent some time in the skies over Southeast Asia a decade before. The initial F-4Ds that arrived in Fargo were the oldest flying F-4Ds in the entire USAF and had been previously assigned to the 49th Tactical Fighter Wing (TFW) at Holloman AFB, New Mexico; 388th TFW at Hill AFB, Utah; and the 48th TFW at RAF Lakenheath, UK. Similar to the F-101B, the Hooligans only had one year to get acclimated to their new aircraft before being put to the test during William Tell 1978. While the team did not earn any top honors, it did learn that the F-4 was a capable air defense platform. For the next 13 years, the Happy Hooligans flew the F-4s from Fargo. In addition, the unit also had its first overseas deployment in 1984 to Naval Air Station Keflavik, Iceland. In 1986, the 178th took part in Creek Klaxon, which saw the North Dakota, Minnesota, and California fighter-interceptor squadrons take over the continuous alert force at Ramstein AB, West Germany, while the resident active Air Force units stationed there transitioned from the F-4 Phantom to the General Dynamics F-16 Fighting Falcon. The F-4Ds maintained the continuous two-ship 24-hours-a-day, seven-days-a-week alert throughout the 1980s and were the last Hooligan fighter aircraft to perform that duty, which had been instituted during the F-51D era more than 40 years prior. In April 1990, with the new General Dynamics F-16s already starting to arrive in Fargo, the last of the F-4Ds left for the final time. The sole F-4D to remain was 64-0972, which was mounted on poles in front of the old main entrance.

F-101B (tail No. 57-0280) and F-4D Phantom II (tail No. 64-0973) stand side by side on the flight line at the NDANG base in 1977. Phantom 0973 had last served with the 492nd TFS, 48th TFW at RAF Lakenheath before coming to Fargo. It was the first F-4 to arrive, still wearing the distinct Southeast Asia camouflage pattern.

Force generation exercises of all F-4 aircraft on the NDANG base were common in the 1980s. Aircraft maintenance personnel would quickly and safely install external fuel tanks, service aircraft, and load weapons, and the aircraft would taxi and simulate launch. White AIM-7 and AIM-9 missiles can be seen on racks before loading.

A Happy Hooligan F-4 is seen from the perspective of a tanker boom operator during aerial refueling.

NDANG members Master Sgt. Philip Poe, Sgt. Brian Self, Senior Airman Randy Grondahl, and Tech. Sgt. Greg Plath made up the first-place weapons load team in the F-4 category at the 1981 Air Defense, Tactical Air Command (ADTAC) Weapons Loading Competition at Tyndall AFB, Florida. It is not known if this photograph was taken at that time, but at least some members of the team can be seen here loading missiles on F-4 aircraft

NDANG members, from left to right, Tech. Sgt. Robert Nysveen, Capt. Ron Saeger, 1st Lt. Thomas Larson, Richard McGuire, and Michael Sauvageau celebrate the aircrew successfully shooting a PQM-102 drone with an AIM-7 missile during the 1980 William Tell fighter competition at Tyndall AFB. The PQM-102 was a full-sized F-102 drone, programmed to be a target for manned fighters, with scores given for hit proximity. Direct hits were rare.

Firefighters of the 119th Civil Engineer Squadron simulate removing an unconscious pilot from an F-4 cockpit during training.

A Happy Hooligan T-33 training aircraft and F-4 Phantom can be seen flying together in this 1980s photograph.

Large snow drifts are in front of the NDANG headquarters in February 1984. NDANG members responded to Gov. Allen Olson's direction to aid civilians stranded by a killer blizzard at 11:00 p.m. on February 4, 1984. Lt. Col. Donald Caswell set up a command post in the office of the 119th Civil Engineering Flight. He directed the rescue efforts of 24 members of that organization. They made 12 trips, traveled 250 miles, and worked 312 man-hours. As a result, they rescued 85 people and most likely saved the lives of 15 others. A total of 23 people died in the storm, with four of the deaths occurring on Nineteenth Avenue in North Fargo.

The 1984 NDANG first-place William Tell F-4 load team is pictured with their trophy. From left to right are Staff Sgt. Larry Gilleland, Sgt. Brian Rook, Tech. Sgt. Greg Plath, and Sgt. Monte Bachmann.

A Happy Hooligan F-4 Phantom (left) flies in formation with F-4s from Minnesota and California over Germany in 1986. The 119th Fighter Group became the first core unit to assume the USAF Zulu alert mission at Ramstein AFB, Germany, referred to as "Creek Klaxon." The 119th and other air defense units stood on continuous alert for one year, providing air sovereignty in Europe for NATO during the Cold War with the Soviet Union. Hohenzollern Castle between the towns of Hechingen and Bisingen can be seen at right.

This is a very unique photograph of two Happy Hooligan F-4 aircraft near a training cruise missile. The NDANG was one of several units staging out of Canadian Forces Base Cold Lake, Canada, attempting to intercept the cruise missile as a test. The missile was launched from a B-52 off the Pacific coast of Canada and the Hooligan F-4s managed to spot and intercept the target for a successful test.

A Happy Hooligan F-4 intercepts a Russian TU-95 Soviet Bear bomber over the Arctic Ocean in 1984. The NDANG deployed to Keflavik, Iceland, that year, where Happy Hooligan pilots intercepted eight Russian bombers. Hooligan pilots also intercepted Bear bombers in 1988 while on alert in Massachusetts.

A Happy Hooligan F-4 fires an AIM-7 missile during a training flight over the Gulf of Mexico during one of several Gulfport, Mississippi, deployments for training in the 1980s.

Three Happy Hooligan F-4s are refueling from a KC-10 tanker in 1987. The photograph was taken by Maj. Larry Harrington, a 178th Fighter Squadron WSO, from the back seat of an F-4 flown by Col. Wally Hegg. Harrington won a Kodak Gallery Award, which was one of 200 given out by Eastman Kodak that year. Only one from each state is selected in four categories for the year.

First Lt. Jeff Aafedt, pilot (left), and Tech. Sgt. Larry Nelson, crew chief, work during an integrated combat turn (ICT) load at the 1986 William Tell competition at Tyndall AFB, Florida. Aafedt was the son of LeRoy Aafedt, who was killed in a T-33 crash in May 1975.

The 1986 William Tell F-4 category champion aircrew is pictured here; from left to right are (first row) Field McConnell, Bill Dittmer, Lyle Andvik, and Tom Larson; (second row) Bernie Kring, Mike Johnson, Gunther Neumann, and Tim Weaver; (third row) Bob Wedberg and Jeff Aafedt. Larson and Weaver were profile three winners in 1984 and 1986 in the F-4 category.

The 1986 William Tell load team champions are seen here; from left to right are Sgt. Monte Bachmann, Staff Sgt. Kevin Nelson, Sgt. Brian Rook, and Airman 1st Class Loren Janke. Rook and Bachmann were also part of the 1984 William Tell load team champions in the F-4 Category, along with Staff Sgt. Larry Gilleland and Tech. Sgt. Greg Plath.

NDANG pilot 1st Lt. Robert Becklund (right) sits with the De Le Pena family at a press conference following the successful heart transplant for infant Andrew De Le Pena, sitting on his father Steven's lap, as his mother, Deborah, interacts with Andrew in December 1986. Steve and Karen McCann made the lifesaving decision to donate their son Michael McCann's organs, which Lieutenant Becklund flew to Moffett Naval Air Station, California, in an NDANG F-4, authorized by Maj. Gen. Alexander Macdonald, the North Dakota adjutant general.

On March 3, 1988, Maj. James "J.D." Nelson, 178th Fighter Squadron pilot, completed a training sortie surpassing 4,000 flying hours in an F-4 Phantom at the NDANG. According to McDonnell Douglas Corporation, only 24 aircrew had accumulated that many flying hours in the aircraft at the time. Nelson started accumulating his F-4 flight hours in 1968 during two tours in Vietnam.

NDANG members from various functional areas on base pose for a photograph in front of the blue centennial F-4 aircraft in 1989. The F-4 received a special paint application in commemoration of the 100th anniversary of the State of North Dakota and the Happy Hooligans' 50,000 accident-free flying hours in the F-4D in 1989.

Four Happy Hooligan F-4s fly in a diamond formation at the 1986 Fargo AirSho. During a presentation at the Fargo Air Museum, North Dakota native and former US Navy Blue Angels boss Capt. Gil Rud said, "even the Blues were impressed by the Hooligans' demonstration."

Tech. Sgt. Brian Self works on an F-4 engine at the NDANG base. The tremendous Happy Hooligan flying safety record can be credited largely to the meticulous care of the aircraft by the 119th aircraft maintenance squadron personnel, like Self, who eventually became a chief master sergeant before his retirement in 2011.

Lt. Col. Thomas "Tommy T" Tolman, the NDANG Kingsley Field, Oregon, alert detachment commander (right), and Richard "Dick" Gabe walk to a flight debrief at the NDANG after completing an F-4 flight. The NDANG maintained its first permanently manned geographically separated alert detachment at Kingsley Field, near Klamath Falls, Oregon, on Oct. 1, 1989. It had two F-4 aircraft standing by 24 hours per day with aircrew rotating in from the Fargo base for short temporary duty periods. The F-4s were replaced by F-16s when the NDANG converted aircraft in 1990.

This Happy Hooligan F-4 received a special paint application in commemoration of the 100th anniversary of the State of North Dakota and the Happy Hooligans' 50,000 accident-free flying hours in the F-4D in 1989.

The blue North Dakota centennial F-4 aircraft can be seen flying near the USAF Thunderbird demonstration team F-16 aircraft at the 1989 Fargo AirSho.

From left to right, Maj. Jim Kapitan, the 119th Security Police Flight commander; Staff Sgt. Allen Albright; and Sgt. Debra (Mahon) Matter pose with the Air National Guard Outstanding Police Unit Jack Lykes Trophy presented to the NDANG on December 1, 1989. Kapitan was the outstanding security commander of the year for the ANG in 1988, and Capt. Teresa Luthi McDonough was the Security Forces Company Grade Officer of the Year in 2006.

Eight

THE FINAL MISSION WITH THE F-16A FIGHTING FALCON

In April 1990, after the last of the F-4Ds had left Fargo, the 178th FIS became operational in the General Dynamics F-16A Fighting Falcon. These were no ordinary Vipers, however, as they were old A models that had been converted to the air defense variant. The 178th was one of just a handful of units to fly these F-16s and was actually the longest-flying F-16A ADF unit in the entire USAF. From September to October 1994, the 178th participated in the 1994 William Tell weapons competition and came in first place with the F-16A ADF. That same year, the 119th FW became the first unit assigned to the Western Air Defense Sector to win the Hughes Trophy. This was the second time the Hooligans had won the prestigious trophy, with the first being in 1974. The Hughes Trophy was awarded to the most outstanding USAF interceptor/tactical fighter squadron with a primary mission in air defense. When the Hooligans won it for the second time in 1994, they were also the first F-16 unit in the entire Air Force to win it.

It was also during the Hooligans' time in the F-16 that they made history in one of the darkest days in American history. Prior to September 11, 2001, the NDANG had maintained an alert detachment at Langley AFB, Virginia. The primary role of the 178th while there was escorting Russian Tu-95 Bear heavy bombers down the coast as they made their way to Cuba. On the morning of September 11, 2001, pilots of the 178th's alert detachment were gearing up for a training sortie when they were informed of a hijacked airliner heading toward the Pentagon. Three NDANG F-16s were scrambled in an attempt to intercept the airliner. Sadly, they were too late to prevent the airliner from hitting the Pentagon, but the NDANG was the first unit to fly top cover over the capital.

During BRAC (Base Realignment and Closure) in 2005, it was decided that the 119th Wing would become home to a remotely piloted aircraft (RPA) unit, utilizing the General Atomics MQ-1B Predator unmanned aerial vehicle (UAV). In January 2007, the last of the 178th's F-16As departed Fargo for the final time. This "Fini" flight of the F-16s brought 50 years of the fighter mission to a close in Fargo.

One of the first NDANG F-16s flies with one of the last NDANG F-4s during an aircraft conversion for the Happy Hooligans in May 1990.

This special Theodore Roosevelt tail marking was applied to F-16A No. 82-0926 shortly after it was converted to the air defense variant and delivered to the Happy Hooligans in the early 1990s. While impressive, it would eventually be replaced by a smaller version that was located just behind the cockpit with the phrase "North Dakota, Roughrider Country" alongside it. F-16A No. 82-0926 is now on display in the memorial airpark on base.

Happy Hooligan C-130B Hercules aircrew and maintainers hold a North Dakota flag prior to the aircraft's departure for the last time on June 30, 1992. The C-130B had approximately 2,550 flying hours, involving 1,352 sorties and carrying 10,247 passengers and 1,150 tons of cargo, including trucks, HUMVEEs, high explosives, satellite communications gear, medical supplies, helicopters, and more during its five and a half years at the NDANG.

A Happy Hooligan C-26 aircraft is refueled on the flight line of the NDANG base. The C-26 served as somewhat of a personnel transport replacement aircraft for the C-130. The C-26 arrived at the NDANG in 1992 and left in 1997. To the pilots, it was known as the "San Antonio sewer pipe" because it was manufactured in San Antonio, Texas, and had a cramped fuselage. On August 14, 1997, the C-26 left the NDANG for San Antonio, ending 50 years of the operational support airlift program for the NDANG.

Maj. Gen. Alexander Macdonald, the North Dakota adjutant general, center, places a US Air Force outstanding unit ribbon on the NDANG organizational flag staff during a ceremony at the NDANG base, as Col. Mike Haugen, the 119th Fighter Wing commander stands behind him on the right on June 5, 1993. It was the fourth Air Force Outstanding Unit Award earned by the NDANG. Haugen was the North Dakota adjutant general from 2000 until 2006.

Brig. Gen. Keith Bjerke, the North Dakota adjutant general, holds up the 1993 John J. Pesch Flying Safety Trophy, which was presented to the NDANG at the National Guard Association of the United States (NGAUS) convention in Boston, Massachusetts, in September 1994. The John J. Pesch Award was given to the two units demonstrating the highest standards of flying safety. The unit also received the Distinguished Flying Unit Plaque at the conference. Bjerke was the adjutant general from 1993 to 2000.

NDANG pilots accept the trophy for overall top team at the 1994 William Tell competition at Tyndall Air Force Base, Florida, on October 21, 1994. From right to left are Capt. Rick "Gibby" Gibney; Maj. Robert "Pee Wee" Edlund; Gen. John M. Loh, the Air Combat Command commander; Maj. Robert "B Squared" Becklund; Maj. George "Flat Top" Lambirth; and Northwest Air Defense Sector weapons controllers Capt. Joseph Bradbury and Capt. Daniel Talbot.

Maj. Robert "Pee Wee" Edlund holds up his third-place Top Gun trophy as team members cheer for him at the William Tell competition banquet on October 21, 1994.

From left to right, members of the 1994 William Tell weapons load team Tech. Sgt. Kevin Nelson, Staff Sgt. Doug Faldet, and Staff Sgt. Shannon Johnson load an AIM-9 Sidewinder missile onto the wing-tip launcher of an NDANG F-16 aircraft during the William Tell rally day on the Hector Field flight line on September 8, 1994. The rally day included a demonstration of the William Tell flying profiles and exercises the team would encounter at the worldwide air-to-air jet fighter contest held at Tyndall AFB October 11–22 that year. The Hooligan "loadeo" team placed second.

NDANG airmen from the 119th Fighter Wing Happy Hooligans win the prestigious Hughes Trophy, which recognizes the most outstanding air-to-air unit in the US Air Force. From left to right are Brig. Gen. Thomas Hruby; Maj. Gen. Phil Killey, 1st Air Force commander; Maj. Gen. Keith Bjerke; a representative from McDonnell Douglas; Col. Michael J. Haugen; and Maj. Gen. Donald Shepperd, director of the Air National Guard, in August 1995.

Flight operations in Fargo had to continue throughout the snowy winter months, and it was common throughout unit history for the 119th Civil Engineer Squadron to remove snow at all hours to maintain the flying schedule. An NDANG F-16 is on the flight line as snow removal equipment blows snow out of the way for operations.

A formation of Happy Hooligan F-16s flies over the International Peace Gardens at the border of North Dakota and Canada on August 22, 1995. The small lakes of North Dakota's Turtle Mountains can be seen in the background.

Seen here is the 1996 William Tell team photograph at the NDANG base prior to the competition at Tyndall AFB. It was the last time the Happy Hooligans would compete in the event.

Members of the NDANG who participated on the 1996 first-place Air National Guard loadeo team are, from left to right, Senior Airman Stephen Crawford, Master Sgt. Kevin Nelson, and Staff Sgt. Charles Renville.

NDANG F-16s fly over the 1997 Fargo AirSho as the US Navy Blue Angels flight demonstration team awaits its turn to fly.

The Happy Hooligans celebrate their 50th anniversary at the newly constructed Heritage Park during the unit training assembly on September 13, 1997. Heritage Park is the home to static aircraft that the NDANG has flown throughout its history.

Airman 1st Class Kathleen Shasky stands ready to direct traffic near an earthen flood levee in the south Fargo Rose Creek neighborhood near drain 27 during the historic 1997 flood fight. Domestic Operations (DOMOPS) in response to natural and man-made disasters at the discretion of the governor are a big part of the National Guard mission, and the NDANG has been activated many times for state emergencies.

Base engineer Maj. Gary Sorlie (left) and Chief Master Sgt. Terry Jacobson, both of the 119th Civil Engineer Squadron, hold the 1996 William L. Deneke Award as the Air Force Reserve Command Outstanding Civil Engineering Unit of the Year during a presentation ceremony on October 4, 1997.

Capt. Mike Depree pilots an NDANG F-16A over the island of Curacao in February 1999. The NDANG was participating in ANG counter-drug operation Coronet Nighthawk, flying missions out of Curacao because of its location between South America and the United States. Coronet Nighthawk involved the use of rotational deployments in support of operations to intercept possible drug trafficking aircraft, starting with deployments to Panama in 1991, for the NDANG.

Master Sgt. Ronald "Rocky" Brovold, of the 119th Maintenance Squadron propulsion element, operates controls of an aircraft engine test facility, better known as the "hush house," at the NDANG base on March 29, 2001. Brovold is doing a full-throttle analysis of a Pratt & Whitney F-16 engine to verify its performance.

Maj. Brad Derrig flies F-16A No. 82-1006 and Maj. Dave Hill flies F-16A No. 82-0929 during an early morning CAP mission over the Pentagon on November 11, 2001. On September 11, 2001, NDANG Alert Detachment 1 F-16s scrambled in response to the terrorist attacks on the World Trade Center in New York City and the Pentagon in Washington, DC, and continued to fly combat air patrol (CAP) missions until the spring of 2002. A gap in the Pentagon where American Airlines Flight 77 crashed into it can be seen.

Lt. Col. Tom "TLAR" Larson holds up a plaque for 60,000 flying hours without a class-A accident in the F-16 during a ceremony at the NDANG on June 7, 2003, as (from left to right) Col. Randy Herman, the 119th Support Group commander; Lt. Col. Rick Gibney; and Col. Rick Utecht, the 119th Fighter Wing commander look on. The NDANG later became the only organization to fly 70,000 hours in the F-16A without a class-A accident. It flew for 16 years and over 45,000 sorties.

Following the September 11, 2001, terrorist attack, the Happy Hooligans began deploying to Southwest Asia regularly. In this photograph, Maj. Gen. Michael J. Haugen, North Dakota adjutant general (far right), visits 119th Security Forces Squadron personnel in Iraq on November 24, 2003. From left to right are Staff Sgt. Rebecca S. (Schneider) Stutz, Staff Sgt. Gavin W. Johnson, Staff Sgt. Michael W. Stutz, Tech. Sgt. Dominic A. Cook, Tech. Sgt. Jason R. Wadell, Tech. Sgt. Gregory S. Goodman, Staff Sgt. Jason R. Coalwell, and Major General Haugen.

From left to right, US senator Kent Conrad, artist Rick Herter, and US congressman Earl Pomeroy discuss Herter's painting *First Pass, Defenders Over Washington* of a Happy Hooligan F-16 flying over the Pentagon on September 11, 2001, during a dedication ceremony of the painting at the Pentagon on September 4, 2002. The painting is on permanent display at the Pentagon.

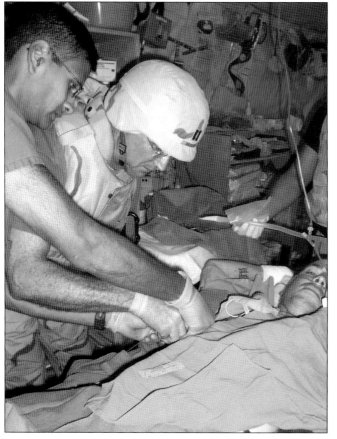

Happy Hooligan Lt. Col. Brian "Slurpy" Sivertson fires an AIM-7M Sparrow medium-range air-to-air missile from an F-16A Fighting Falcon at a BQM-34A "Firebee" sub-scale aerial target drone over the Gulf of Mexico during Combat Archer, an air-to-air Weapons System Evaluation Program (WSEP) at Tyndall AFB, Florida, on October 7, 2003.

Capt. Dwight Harley, a physician assistant with the 119th Medical Group (wearing helmet), performs a medical procedure in the emergency room while on deployment at Joint Base Balad, Iraq, on November 17, 2005. As of 2022, the NDANG contributed over 2,600 personnel for deployments in support of the continuing Global War on terrorism, which began September 11, 2001.

From left to right, Maj. Gen. Mike Haugen, the North Dakota adjutant general; Col. Robert Becklund, the 119th Fighter Wing commander; and Maj. Allen Albright examine the proposed Department of Defense BRAC planning documents at NDANG on May 13, 2005. The BRAC recommendation for the NDANG was to realign Hector International Airport Air Guard Station, North Dakota, and for the 119th Fighter Wing's 15 F-16s to retire. It was a process that evolved and eventually resulted in the NDANG conversion to C-21 aircraft and the MQ-1 remotely piloted aircraft missions.

NDANG leaders and key 119th Logistics Readiness Squadron (LRS) members accept the ANG Daedalian Maj. Gen. Warren R. Carter Logistics Effectiveness Award for fiscal year 2003 at an LRS conference in Reno, Nevada, on April 5, 2004. Other major awards for LRS in the F-16 era included the American Petroleum Institute award in 1994, 2002, and 2004.

Capt. Jason M. Tautfest, 178th Fighter Squadron, shows the first "Pilot for the Day," John Murphy, the inner workings of an NDANG F-16 on August 30, 2005. Regrettably, Murphy succumbed to his battle with cancer on September 18, 2005. Tautfest initiated the program at the NDANG. As honored guests, pilots for the day were given the rank of brigadier general and were provided a special interactive tour of the base.

Seen here is one of several tent cities erected by 119th Civil Engineer Squadron members to house US military personnel staying at the Gulfport Combat Readiness Training Site, Mississippi, in support of the Hurricane Katrina relief effort on September 15, 2005. The ANG response to disasters is a key role in domestic operations. DOMOPS are state missions supporting civil authorities at the direction of the governor in times of crisis. The governor is the commander of the ANG in each state.

Lt. Col. Craig "Merkin" Schroeder (left) and Maj. David "Jams" Winjum (right) spray carbonated liquid at Lt. Col. John Dougherty upon the completion of his Fini (final) flight at the NDANG base on March 13, 2006. Fini flights were common leading up to the F-16's permanent departure from the NDANG in 2007.

Capt. Stephanie L. Kelsen, a 178th Fighter Squadron pilot, prepares for the flight that put her into a select group of female pilots to surpass 1,000 flight hours in the F-16 on August 19, 2006. Captain Kelsen is the only woman in the North Dakota Air National Guard to reach the milestone in a fighter aircraft.

Happy Hooligan F-16 pilots gather for the last group photograph before the F-16s, and many of the pilots, departed the unit to continue flying fighters at NDANG on May 6, 2006. Pilots of the 178th Fighter Squadron are, from left to right, Maj. Jon "Bullwinkle" Wutzke, Lt. Col. William "Kid" Pallen, Lt. Col. Cecil "Bud" Hensel Jr., Maj. Dean "Otis" Eckman, Lt. Col. Brian "Slurpy" Sivertson, Lt. Col. Kent "Q-tip" Olson, Capt. Stephanie "Vapor" Kelsen, Lt. Col. Mike "Spike" Nelson, 1st Lt. Ryan "Chopper" Rastedt, Capt. Matt "Ninja" Kiser, Col. Robert "B-Squared" Becklund, Lt. Col. Wayne "Shark" Tranby, Maj. Jason "Trout" Tautfest, Lt. Col. Rick "Calvin" Omang, Maj. Craig "Merkin" Schroeder, Lt. Col. John "Mongo" Dougherty, Lt. Col. Dana "Mule" Mullenhour, Capt. Joshua "Opie" Carlson, Maj. David "Jams" Winjum, Capt. Nicholas "Waldo" Zetocha, and 1st Lt. Chris "Demo" Domitrovich.

Members of the 119th Medical Group administer vaccinations to civilians as part of USAF Medflag 06 in Accra, Ghana, on September 11, 2006. North Dakota governor John Hoeven and Maj. Gen. Michael Haugen, the North Dakota adjutant general, announced North Dakota's intent to form a state part-partnership program (SPP) with the Republic of Ghana at a news conference at the NDANG on August 12, 2004. The North Dakota National Guard SPP eventually expanded to include the African countries of Togo and Benign.

Members of the 119th Aircraft Maintenance Squadron gather for a photograph with remaining F-16s on the flight line at the NDANG base on October 27, 2006. The F-16s began to depart for the boneyard in Arizona following this photograph, until the last one left in February 2007.

Lt. Col. Scott "Poacher" Lysford pilots an NDANG F-16 with a wingman on both sides over the snow-covered fields of North Dakota on January 12, 2007.

Three F-16s from the 119th Fighter Wing of the NDANG are refueled by a 319th Air Refueling Wing KC-135 over North Dakota prior to departing for Tucson to be retired to the boneyard on January 16, 2007.

Senior Airman Jeffrey J. Jacobson is working near F-16 tail No. 980 as he notices a problem that delays the departure of the aircraft from the NDANG base to AMARC on January 30, 2007. Capt. Ryan L. Rastedt, 178th Fighter Squadron, sits in the cockpit. Jacobson noticed that the hydraulic lines were jumping, which is a sign that something was wrong with the aircraft. For aborting the flight and preventing a potential mishap, he was later awarded the 119th Wing Outstanding Safety Award for 2007.

Capt. Stephanie L. Kelsen, 178th Fighter Squadron, pilots an NDANG F-16 alongside one of the first C-21 (Learjet) aircraft to join the Happy Hooligan ranks as it flies into Fargo on January 10, 2007. Lt. Col. Craig R. Schroeder and Maj. Jon R. Wutzke, also both of the 178th Fighter Squadron, are flying the C-21 as it arrives in Fargo for the first time. The C-21 was considered a "bridge mission" until approximately 2010, when it was expected to be replaced by the new C-27 Joint Cargo Aircraft (JCA), which was mothballed before delivery. The NDANG 177th Airlift Squadron earned the 2009 Joint Operational Support Airlift Center (JOSAC) outstanding squadron of the year in the C-21.

NDANG members operate the controls of an unmanned aerial systems (UAS) MQ-1 Predator from an aircraft ground control station (GCS) in Fargo on June 27, 2007. While the disappearance of the fighter mission was disappointing to many, the importance of the Predator mission made up for it. The unit became a 24-hours-a-day, seven-days-a-week operational organization contributing to the nation's defense and war efforts on a daily basis, a highly rewarding mission.

NDANG pilots began flying MQ-1 flights around the world from Fargo in April 2007, but it took several more years for training flights to begin locally, with the 119th Launch and Recovery Element (LRE) initially being located at the Grand Forks AFB. Here NDANG aircraft maintenance personnel run the first 119th LRE engine tests on a Happy Hooligan MQ-1 aircraft at the Grand Forks AFB on September 25, 2012.

Each Happy Hooligan static fighter aircraft and an operational F-16 aircraft were gathered on the flight line at the NDANG in preparation for permanent display at Heritage Park in 1997. The aircraft pictured here represent more than 60 years of service to the United States in the fighter mission in some of the harshest weather imaginable. The NDANG had an unequaled flying safety record of 144,763.1 hours and 97,710 sorties without a class-A mishap in fighter aircraft from 1973 to 2007. It had another 4,389 hours and 3,484 sorties in the T-33. No other F-16 unit matched the Hooligans' 72,293.3 hours and 46,763 sorties without a class-A mishap as of 2007. The accomplishments of the North Dakota Air National Guard are impressive by any standards. All of the accomplishments and contributions by unit members during the fighter aircraft era could not be included in this book. The organization has played a large part in developing civilian and community leaders in the region and military leaders for the national defense. This book is an attempt to honor those people.

DISCOVER THOUSANDS OF LOCAL HISTORY BOOKS
FEATURING MILLIONS OF VINTAGE IMAGES

Arcadia Publishing, the leading local history publisher in the United States, is committed to making history accessible and meaningful through publishing books that celebrate and preserve the heritage of America's people and places.

Find more books like this at
www.arcadiapublishing.com

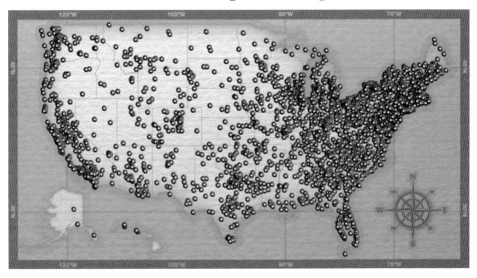

Search for your hometown history, your old stomping grounds, and even your favorite sports team.